FEEDING THE FIRE

ALSO BY TWYLA M. HANSEN

Rock • Tree • Bird

Dirt Songs: A Plains Duet
(with Linda M. Hasselstrom)

Prairie Suite: A Celebration
(with Paul A. Johnsgard)

Potato Soup

Sanctuary Near Salt Creek

In Our Very Bones

How to Live in the Heartland

FEEDING
THE
FIRE

Poems

Twyla M. Hansen

Twyla M. Hansen
Nebraska State Poet
2013-2018

WSC PRESS - *Wayne, NE*

ISBN 978-1-7379241-2-8
Published by WSC Press

Edited by David Z. Drees
Layout design by Chad Christensen
Cover design by Tyler Pecena

Author photo by Bryce E. Darling

Front cover © 2016 Madelyne Hansen, Outgrowth.
Screen print over monoprint on Stonehenge paper 23 x 30 in.

WSC Press
1111 Main Street
Wayne, NE 68787

wscpress@wsc.edu
WSCPRESS.COM

—to Steve, Joei, Kathleen, Maddy

In loving memory of
Thomas Murphy Hansen
(1948-2018)

CONTENTS

THREE

FEEDING noun
1 : the act or process of eating or being fed
2 : an instance of feeding
Synonyms: Nourishing, fueling, filling, sustaining, providing, giving

FIRE noun
1a
(1) : the phenomenon of combustion manifested in light, flame, and heat
(2) : one of the four elements of the alchemists air, water, fire, and earth
1b
(1) : burning passion
(2) : liveliness of imagination
Also: One of the five classic elements: water, earth, fire, air, ether (space)

Merriam-Webster, Roget's Thesaurus, Wikipedia

Help us to be the always hopeful
gardeners of the spirit
who know that without darkness
nothing comes to birth
as without light
nothing flowers.

—May Sarton

ONE

So Easy in Fall

So easy in fall
to fall in love
in love of wind
the winds of fall

the blowsy scents
warm cool in-between
warm and cool battle
the season's whims

on a whim outing walk
with me on the prairie
walk the warm hilltops
step into the cool ravines

before us the native grass
turns red gold purple
the late season forbs
bend their heads

wind and clouds stir
birds skirr the sky
the calls and responses
from somewhere close

come lie with me dear
where deer have rested
on thatch rest your bones
we are here close your eyes

breathe the soil the drought
the rain the green the brown
overhead seedheads wave
that other world can wait

Five Decades in the Same Place

This house is a rock surrounded by layers of green,
a foundation for the living above and below ground.

At first light, I contemplate all the lives and losses
riffling among the leaves and roots, the emptiness
now indoors pressing heavy against my days.

July, filled with its triggers: generations of family dinners,
birthday celebrations, kiddy pool parties, the playhouse,
the overnight gaggles. The past, ever present.

The multiple additions, the plantings planned and not,
scores of wings, paws, and feet. Deaths by tooth, claw,
disease. Pets buried, a handful of human ashes spread.

How many other lives thrived on this land long before
me? After fifty years, it's not the same house, not the same
yard, I'm no longer the same person.

Dew floats up, adrift in another sticky day. Off to the north,
miles from here, rain clouds irrigate the cornfields.
Bird songs and chatters upend the silence, and across the fence,

a neighbor yells at his dog, loose again. Fully caffeinated,
I plan my morning, my day, my life. I inhale the strength
of this generous and watery planet. I am alive. Alive.

Each Morning

I open the glass door to the dark
invite in the thicket   quiet but for leaf-flaps
while sun slides up slow

I cannot distinguish between multiple dim trunks
and the duff below turning to compost   that everyday
decay   its silent music

And just beyond
is the pile where I invite small furred ones to feast
overnight on food scraps

Soon the first calls of jays   *Hey! Hey!*
wake-up to those still here   Most have flown   pulled
by the magnetic field   the loss of light which

our bones comprehend
Their leaving like other multiple departures we do not always
notice   Over the years they pile up like leaves   each one diving

to its bright death   Yet here each morning the day turns
brighter   Each bird brings me sustenance as they wing
their way to my world

Into the Night

I've always loved perennials, the succession of blooms
through the seasons, and this spring when I renovated
entire beds, they somehow filled the empty spaces
inside me as I dug out the overgrown herbs and vines,
those that occupied too much real estate in my life.

And when I made room in other beds for different
perennials, searched for just the right plants, planned
their spacings, bloom periods, hardiness, colors and
heights, I knelt in thankfulness for the process.

Those empty spaces at times call to me after I work
outside, am inside at last light, and exhale as the sun
drops below the horizon. Light softens, covers this corner
of earth with a blanket of yellow, peach, amber, reduces
the volume of aloneness until it disappears into the night.

Late March, Full Moon

When I open my blinds, the setting moon is still high in the west,
lighting my wild yard when I take food scraps to the compost pile,
lay my small offerings on the table of a new day.

This is the gaunt season, in between winter and actual spring,
when songbirds arrive and others depart, when leaves have
yet to unfold and mask this acre's many imperfections.

Just as I try to hide my flaws. I will spare you the chambers
of solitude I inhabit, those I step into and without warning
wilt in self-pity. I'm trying to live more in the moment.

Like the lifeless pines in my backyard that are still upright,
their bare arms outstretched, gathering the wind. Today's
forecast is a red flag of gusts and heat and low humidity.

So I do what the living must do: lug buckets of water
to the new shrubs I planted, note the numerous piles
of limbs and brush, the sprouting invasive weeds.

On this cusp of dark and light, the moon fades as the sun
beams up. Then all my surroundings—soil, woods, sorrows—
merge into morning, and a fox runs through it.

I Never Thought I'd Outlive
My Evergreens

We planted them along the north lot line,
a seedling windbreak all we could afford,
where cocklebur, sandbur, thistle all thrived
and brome grew taller than those tiny pines.

My father and his father planted trees,
carried water, hope, love through drought years
to slow the wind, shade the farmhouse. Later,
my brothers and I climbed to new heights.

This small woods on city's edge likewise
branched. Kids thrived beneath shades of green,
while disease, drought, time plodded on.
Alone now, I replant with natives.

I'm blue when the living must depart, but my
hope and love, once planted, never die.

All the Stars We Cannot See

On the oak branch, early morning, two male cardinals
land. One hops to the feeder, takes a seed, cracks
the shell, feeds his offspring.

This goes on all morning with a multitude of feathers.

Sometimes I wonder what will happen to this untamed place
when I am no longer here. Will someone decide to clear
the oaks, level the evergreens, yank the wildflowers?

This acre is surrounded by chem-laden carpets of lawn.
There are fewer songbirds and pollinators, we've polluted
our waters, abused the soil, heated the planet.

It would be so easy to give up.

Nature wasn't built in a day. Neither was this natural yard,
with its limb-tangle nests, wood-pile insects, tall and ground-
level green things both human- and creature-planted.

Uncertainty swirls around this tiny refuge. Overhead,
all the stars we cannot see are constant. With or without
us, in some form or another, the earth will carry on.

April Fool

morning and I don't see the cardinals yet and the damn squirrels
are gobbling the black oil sunflower seeds I just scattered under
the oak because it was 29 overnight and food is not yet plentiful

in the wild which my yard is and I want those beauties with their
conical beaks and cone heads and red-reddish-buff bodies to make
more babies and nest somewhere in my densest evergreens

this yard a habitat an oasis surrounded with lifeless lawns
and here more species of flora and fauna above and below
ground you can shake a stick at which is what I do when

the neighbor's cat wanders into it and scatters the birds and I'm so
committed to nourishing them that when I'm ready to step outside in
an attempt to tame this place a bit I first check for birds at my feeders

and so you see why I don't get as much work done as I'm either staring
at them when I work indoors or hoping I don't disturb them while they're
filling their lovely bodies at the feeders when I have serious stuff

to do out there even though I know they will return after I retreat inside
and I can't change the direction this planet is headed in changing climate
but I can focus on keeping my birds safe productive happy here right now

The Finch

His yellow warmth fills my palm: neck broken,
eyes closed, feathers splayed, legs folded.
He weighs almost nothing.

The glass shows an outline, waxy, of head,
outstretched wings, tail feathers.

I stroke his breast. I carry my grief beneath
the evergreen, whisper *I'm sorry. I'm so very sorry.*

We invite the outdoors into our home
through tall windows; all birds see is blue sky.

As a child, I collected feathers, stroked
my face with hawk tails, fluff as small

as milkweed seed, carried by wind to the path
in the windbreak where it landed at my feet.

So many ways to inflict harm in this world.
I must believe most people mean well.
We must find a way to help the earth.

Orioles

In the afternoon, orioles squabble at the jelly feeder—
black-and-flame males jockey for position at the perch, buff-breasted
females wait—much buzz-calling and flap-winging.

I don't know their reasoning, let's call it—standing motionless
at the glass door—yet witness threads of order: one finishes,
the next one dips into purple sweetness—

grapes that at some great distance were tended, harvested, preserved,
packaged, shipped, shelved, sold, allowing me to step out under
the oak and spoon into the orange feeder.

Did these birds from a great distance sense this unspoiled acre?
They could easily be sipping nectar from trumpet creeper blooms,
the vine I planted now taking over.

The orioles have been here all summer, weaving bulbous nests
in the neighbor's cottonwood, from treetops singing praises
to the day, raise their young.

Now in early September I expect them to leave any time,
as they will at night without warning—*travel safe, my lovelies!* —
winging to some other untamed place.

In a Time of Uncertain Climate

Snow disappears overnight as temperatures
rise in the dark. A low sun

                        bulges between limbs,
exposes dun leaf litter, the twisted bare vines.

Evergreens point their needle-fingers toward
a rotating sky. February,

                        and the loud geese
have gathered, regathered, and taken flight.

A woman wakes after uneasy sleep, tosses
her blankets, stares out

                        to the blank day,
to the unseen exhale, the murmuring earth.

Mid-April on the Plains

Winter wakens after a short nap.
It rises, hungry, to chase and catch
an unlucky prey, clamps hard with teeth
meant to kill, its head shaking from side
to side, the sacrifice's back feet
kicking, releasing its fine flakes and
fur to feed the beast now swirling in
the upper atmosphere. Nature, red
in tooth and claw, aided by humans,
while deniers stand mute.

Wind screams into the danger zone, builds
into blizzard that sweeps down from the
Arctic across the northern Plains, lighted
on the screen in green to blue, purple
to pink as more than a foot of snow
dumps across the landscape. Clouds rule,
bare tree limbs quake, calves still drop
in pastures as moisture sucks up from
the Gulf. And to the south, thunder-gods
rage into funnels.

Afterward, a few lay dead in its
wake—those unlucky prey—both wild
and domestic. We shake our collective
heads, dig our way out, survey damage.
For now, the beast is sated, licking
its blooded chops. Tundra continues
its thaw as the ice sheet melts, altering
ocean currents. Once again, spring comes
on footed claws, sits looking over field
and city, then limps along.

Sea of Green

A drowsy heat hangs heavy over the deep middle,
over the sea of corn and soybean planted on prairie—
once a vast ecosystem, its soil now slowly depleting.

A yellow bi-plane loops over the fields, skims above
center pivots spraying water pumped from the aquifer,
spews a cloud of pest-killers over the crop leaves—

those powerhouses of efficiency and engineering—
using sunlight-water-CO_2 to manufacture energy,
exhale moisture and oxygen above shallow roots.

The steady breeze pulses its syllable—*mono, mono*—
to a flat horizon, the tree-lined river an oasis winding
through the emptied-out Plains. What will happen

when the water is gone? When the heat becomes
unbearable, in this place where prolonged drought
and dirt flying off in wind is but a distant nightmare?

Most travelers on this ribbon of concrete glance at
the waving green below the big sky blue and think
inland ocean, or simply speed on through.

But those caught in the industrial ag scheme—that
deeply vested, non-renewable treadmill—ignore
the future, carry on, inhale these temporary yields.

Another World

Below ground, another world lies cool and
damp, its silence we take for granted, filled
with grit and goodness all living together.

Roots reach down, absorb what they need,
invertebrates worm, wiggle, dig unseen,
mammals are home with bacteria and fungi.

Mostly we ignore our soil, the terra firma
on which we land, then excavate, pave,
poison, mine, deplete, pollute, discard.

When will we minister to this body that
clothes and feeds us, this skin of earth,
the mystery actions over millions of years

that led to its formation? When will we
learn its lost vocabulary, articulate its heart
to a planet filled with such hunger?

Early October

Rain taps its fingers against the skylight. This wooded
and wild-flowered yard is a rain garden, a carbon-sink,
a haven. Leaves decay and build soil above roots.

Day before yesterday, about four dozen monarchs
clustered at day's end on overhanging branches. Early
October: by morning the monarchs had flown.

Lone migrants stop here to feed and rest, and dozens of loud
grackles stab dirt below the oak. A sudden something scatters
them out of sight. A shy cardinal then pecks below the feeders.

A thump at the glass, two feathers waft the air: an unlucky
traveler has broken their neck. I weep for it and the thousands
of others that risk their lives on the long journey.

This is the time of year my life-mate was on his own journey
away, not of his own doing, but from a rotting from within.
I am now in charge here, but only somewhat.

Leaves turn yellow and brown as nights grow long and lonely.
I wake early thinking of the last patch of troublesome weeds,
their flowers transforming into burs that helps them spread.
Behind every ray of joy on this earth lies a shadow of dark.

Under the Sun

This morning, the gray a reminder
of an indifferent world, you rise
each day into a new routine, put off
thinking about that ache

                in the jaw,
the unexpected loss of appetite,
the nightmare in which doors keep
slamming and you are lost.

              Because it's
the unseen particles you can't quite
grasp, isn't it, and beneath your feet
where microscopic fears live,

small-minded creatures undermine
everything you stand for, where
your lost loved ones now reside.
Last night,

          the new moon shrouded
by clouds, Venus barely visible,
you remembered it's also where hope
rises, the seeds you will plant to continue

the green goodness, the reason
to shake off dread, inhale the dampness,
to be present under the sun in order
to do the work before you.

Distant Stars Are Calling to Me

May: the month of remembrance and celebration.
Green things collaborate to color the northern hemisphere,
migrating birds travel in packs across the Plains.

They are navigating by stars, moon, the earth's magnetic field.
We don't understand how exactly they know "home."
We do know what lively wings mean, passing through
our yard to feed and rest, before they move on.

That the rufous-sided towhee stayed this time for three days
instead of one and there's hope the thrasher might be happy here.
Is it possible that this time we paid more attention?
Now, there's definitely more to worry about.

Distant stars are calling to me from beyond the morning clouds.
Mother and father, I'm thinking of you on your birthdays,
those marks on the calendar reminding me how I came to exist.
What would you say now about the land of your parents?

Look out over our remnant prairies where the wild things thrive.
Watch over our towns and cities and fields as wings fly over them.
Help us better see our way beneath your faithful star-gaze.

Field Guide

Late February, and the juncos still scour
for small seeds, still chitter from brush piles
when I step outside in the early dark.

A brutal winter, record snow and cold,
and I wonder how long before the short
cliffs and piled up mounds will disappear.

The sun rises fiery, clouds go blue and pink,
trunks turn yellow and pale. Everything pivots
us forward. Take juncos—the original

snowbirds—in their slate-gray uniforms
and flash-white tailfeathers when they wing
their way to higher latitudes. As I learn

in my well-thumbed *Field Guide to the Birds*,
an inscription in my mother's handwriting
indicating I gave it to Father—my own field guide

to planting, harvest, animal husbandry, the stars—
faded newsprint marking Wrens, Sparrows, Confusing
Fall Warblers, as the seasons of their lives took flight.

Climbing the Mountain

We weren't mountain climbers, not like friends
who regularly scaled Indian Peaks, Spanish Peaks,
Mount Elbert and slept high beneath the stars.

Yet there we were each summer, climbing with others
Medicine Bow Peak after our journey to re-trace trails
along rivers, learning wagon, Chimney Rock, heartbreak,

and into Wyoming with its carvings and wagon ruts,
where the pioneers began the ascent in their effort
to reach the promised coast before winter set in,

where natives thrived for thousands of years in its
snowy mountains and sunny plains in earth lodges
and tipis near waters, before they were forced out.

For us, the mountain was not life or death, even
though with each step we wondered if we'd survive,
12,000 daunting feet reached one huff-step at a time.

And each year was distinct, in thin air balanced
on rocks, the giddiness at the top—*we made it!*
only to scramble down in storms and lightning.

And life is like this, scrambling up one mountain
or another. A few years back, we tried to recreate
that journey, attempted to climb that peak,

but this time there was no guide, no helping
hands to cross the ice fields, no encouragement,
just tedium, the two of us in this alien landscape.

So strange to walk those trails without others
ahead or behind, to hear no voices, no laughs
or calls, *Are you coming? Don't give up!*

Those days and years have long disappeared.
And yet, if I focus just right, I can still see you ahead—
your strength and affection moving me forward.

Cries in the Night

think dog you'd be wrong
more like a hoarse scream
untamed

couple of years ago
shrieks in the dark
unchained

vixen imploring her kits
to come to her
cover?

I stood at the screen frozen
spring screeches
haunting

plaintive calls outside
my house wafted
wilding

after a spell subsided
and surely they heard
mother?

but now near solstice
winter air seeping in
door-cracked

from bed-time dark
howls squeals yowls
unchecked

I hear the disturbing
high wails to attract an
other?

like cries in the night
after our beloveds
depart

never to return
certain as a broken
heart

Black Moon

How do we comprehend our
fascination with lunar phases,
the unknowable nature of humans,
their actions at times beyond us,

given that most of us are planted
on solid ground when we look up,
while others stare into blackness,
then hurtle themselves toward it.

Black Moon—the second new moon
in a month—they say is the evil twin
of a blue moon, the time our young
friend stepped into that darkness.

And last year's phenomenon,
the rare *Super Harvest Blood Moon*
around this time, when the orb slipped
into Earth's deepest shadows, turned

its eerie red face toward us, beckoned,
between the time of its fullness and its
sliver of wax or wane, with predictable
forecasts of doom and gloom.

Once we were on a hill near the river
and the trail disappeared, no longer
maintained, overgrown grass and oaks
on one side, the other a steep drop-off.

But we forged on in hope of viewing
moon's rise, the Milky Way a spiral
with a line of stars in the middle,
what Romans called the *Via Lactea*.

Only the setting sun and shadow's growth
forced us back. We vowed, *next time,*
next year, but unfortunately, we did not.
Indeed, at times our paths can be obscured.

TWO

I Carry the Grief

I carry the grief on my shoulder, like
Atlas holding up the celestial sky.
At times I barely notice, the weight there
I've grown accustomed to next to my neck,
while other times it twists into a pain.
Maybe it's the moon, full again, stirring
tides, making its mischief known internal,
or a drop in barometric pressure.
Or is it Zeus, throwing his thunderbolts?
The world we knew is now forever changed.
Tonight, the flower moon glows upward through
clear sky. I focus on its hopeful face,
the weight lifting up, while all around us,
mystery whirls—unknown, unseen—in silence.

Happiness

The secret to happiness is low expectations.
—Barry Schwartz

This morning I wrap myself with streaming rays of sun,
ponder another day without you.

I did not ask for this. I never expected the ground to give
below my feet, my rock to disappear.

I stare out to the acre we built this house on decades
ago on a weedy pasture.

The fifty-foot oak we planted from an acorn is alive
with birdsong and squirrels,

its roots reaching into soil transforming slowly from
sand and clay to black loam,

its insects and shade and leathery leaves breathing
carbon into oxygen.

Just one of many trees, our many years together,
my heart at the moment buoyant.

Right now, I have trouble imagining the future,
what to expect next,

charting that unfamiliar landscape. I turn instead
my attention to the bird feeders,

the migrants that make their way to our backyard
and raise their young,

intent in their purpose. For now, this is my assignment,
to find each day that

which makes me happy. I inhale my surroundings, each
intake an expectation, a birdsong, rising.

Feeding the Fire

This acre once an overgrazed pasture, a dairy farm
on the city-edge that became a housing development;
we chose the largest parcel, proceeded to build and plant.

Decades later, it's a wooded habitat that mostly belongs
to the wild, with parts impenetrable. Today I'm fighting back:
lopping, gathering, breaking limbs to feed the fire pit.

I think of all the evenings over the years that my husband fed
this very fire. He loved the wood smoke, this back yard,
the fire rings at parks, or wherever we camped. And indoors,

in our woodstove and fireplace. Something about flames
evoked a primal part of himself he couldn't put into words.
Even the gas fireplace in our bedroom, on a frigid night,

filled this need. As if he knew that someday the fire within
would consume him. Did he sense it, the multiple times
we sat out here drinking beer and roasting brats?

Long after I'd retreated into the house, he sat in the dark.
Today, I am burning sticks in an effort to sort out my life,
recall his face. He would have grinned at my ambition.

Garbage, Etc.

once at the small college where I worked
we leveled an area to make a new practice field
and uncovered a cache of buried garbage

used needles, rotted tape, and bandages
what now would be classified as hazardous
but back then just something to ditch

or burn, like at the old landfill on the north edge
of the city, fires of mattresses and tires
and trash reducing to ash, smoke rising, acrid

and at the old insane asylum, as it was called then,
my now-husband and pal shooting rats at that landfill
their .22s aimed between the eyes

imagine that today, two boys on their bikes
with rifles wrapped in their newspaper carrier
bags on the handlebars, crossing town

later, he used a camera instead of ammo
to capture nature, our time together
before the melanoma that metastasized

sometimes change occurs for the better
at others, moves toward the unthinkable
life with its burning, hidden hazards, taking aim

I Wonder What He Is Doing

Now that he is no longer living
I wonder what he is doing—
his spirit, that is—wandering
unseen out in his wood shop
at night amidst his unfinished
projects, the houses pollinators
can lay their eggs in, with holes
of various diameters he drilled
into blocks, native bees filling
first into the back, laying more
eggs, capping the openings with
mud-mucous-grass, brown button
to protect it from predators.
The following spring eaten
out by the larvae. His spirit
looks over the board stacks
scraps screws power tools,
wondering what project
should be next, more picture
frames, perhaps, or start
something hefty, like a bed
frame nightstand cabinet,
something on his list not
started yet but intended.
Instead, his spirit takes him
to something novel, never
tried, an unfolded challenge.
I bet she would appreciate
a puzzle box, cutting sanding
fitting the pieces into place,
so intricate yet strong, his
unseen fingers feeling along
the edges for the clues
she will miss in the dark.

Now That You Are Gone

Now that you are gone, I must amuse myself.
No running jokes, no repeated lines from favorite movies
like *Annie Hall, The Jerk, Monty Python*,
no random non-sequiturs from a moon app.

We can walk to the curb from here.
The new phone book is here, the new phone book is here!
Ain't dead yet!
It's lonely up here.

You'd laugh at my attempts at what is called
almost cooking, pulling out leftovers,
frozen dinners, cans, and packages.
Chips and salsa and beer, call it supper.

I marvel still at your multiple talents,
your instant smart-ass comebacks,
those quick retorts I thought of too late,
your dry wit evident until the end.

What's it going to do, kill me?

I watch orioles jockey at the jelly feeder,
juvenile foxes cavort in our backyard—
these close surroundings a comfort of sorts—
walk out in my pajamas to stare at the moon.

Every Day of Fall Reminds Me of You

Every day of fall reminds me of you.
Late September: I miss you at 6:30
when I wake in the dark, miss your sure steps
toward the kitchen to brew our black coffee.

Late September. I miss you at 6:30,
also lunch time and again at dinner.
In the kitchen I brew my black coffee.
The loss of light was what you disliked most.

Mostly, I eat alone at lunch and dinner,
sometimes at the sink, staring out the window.
The dark season was what you feared the most;
it's fitting you died around the solstice.

Sometimes at the sink, staring out the window
I watch a fox rummaging the compost.
On the solstice, we used to light a fire
to beseech the steady return of light.

The fox comforts me on this lonely path,
as every fall day reminds me of you.
I will again light the solstice fire ring,
watch it spark, piercing light into the dark.

Slant of Light

Together, we stared out back at dusk
to long rays of sun, a yellow highlighter
against the sides of trunks and limbs,
so fragile over the grass field beyond,
our unspoken fears meanwhile on hold.

Like the tender light he sought for photos
with his large-format camera, tucking
his head under the hood, the image upside-
down, focusing, pulling out the back
to expose the film as he thumbed the click.

The exquisite detail in prints laid bare
later in black-and-white, images I view
on these walls—dilapidated motels, empty
gas stations, odd post offices, old structures,
faded signs, tilted, broken, as rural towns
have emptied and fallen into ruin.

He was fascinated with the process of the
man-made returning to earth, just as I can
see now that was where he was headed.
His patience with the camera, this life
of ours, the fire he carried within.

Tonight, I watch until the moment the light
fades, the trees and grass fall into shadow.
How I wish we could share it one more time!
Yet that slant of light he loved is mine
as I search the dark for the evening star.

Borrowed Time

As I look back, you were living on borrowed time,
as if time were a thing deposited in a bank account,
available for withdrawal or debit/credit, neither
concept I understood in spite of accounting 101.

Same as I never quite caught how energy and mass
are interchangeable, different forms of the same thing,
that the equation $E = mc2$ meant so little back then
in high school where we met, in spite of physics.

I wonder if Einstein would have agreed that time,
as they say, is money, that everything in the universe
can be objectified, quantified, and/or capitalized,
even soil/water/air, in spite of their intrinsic good.

How when we learned your cancer had gone internal,
undetected, for many years gathering mass and speed,
until the energy it produced made itself known. Then,
the rush of treatment, the fight, in spite of the odds.

Yet the energy you consumed to defeat the tumor
in your brain that surely traveled the speed of light
squared, in body-years, rendered it useless at the end.
In spite of money/energy/time, you couldn't be saved.

Giving Him Away

Don't call me heroic. By habit, I checked
pockets in his outerwear before donating,
when I could have stuffed in $10s and $20s.
A newspaper-motivating coat drive.

Donating warmth to those in need is kind,
but the act of giving my husband's clothing
took an article in the local news.
Flooded, gutted, like losing him again.

Giving away his used garments is harder
than it sounds. The shopping and gifts, the packed
bags and trips; I'm losing the flood of his scent.
It helps that other men will now be warmed.

This season of songs, shopping, packed memories.
We'll again gather around the lit tree,
while others are warmed with his coats, hats, scarves.
We'll again breakfast with his favorite dishes.

As we unwrap presents under the tree,
we'll miss him. But don't call us heroic with our
habits, overspending, champagne, and privilege.
It's what we call re-learning how to live.

New Year's Day

The decade faded overnight like dry snow.
You died a year ago, toward its end, and
this new one has yet to prove its green show,
the odd weather I try to comprehend.
Last year blew in blizzards, ice storms, bitter cold,
stuck-down grief. I stumbled my way from spring
to heat. See people, stay active, I was told,
discover wild flowers each new day can bring.
In fall, the sky turned red-cool at sundown.
Memories swirled and pummeled me like soft rain.
I scribbled and danced my way through year's brown
end, with hope my heart could expand again.
Last night I dreamed you nearby, standing still.
Then sun dawned. I still hold you; always will.

One Year After

By now, gust-winds have stripped the oaks of the season's garments
and the pines of their annual needle-shedding. I rake those leathered
stiffs onto paths and under tree driplines, leave them for useful insects
to overwinter. I gather twigs, branches, and logs for the solstice bonfire.

This dark season—with all its transition-triggers—gladdens and saddens:
holidays; everyday interactions, our running joke that the longer we were
together, the more alike we became, his presence/absence the two-sided
head of Janus that blew me headlong into an unfamiliar year.

Our old cats are now buried out back. When I take scraps to the compost
pile, earth-scent rises to greet my watered eyes. Wildness continues to strut,
trot, waddle, hoof, and forage through our yard, this wild haven. Even
one year after, today hits me harder than I imagined.

I stuck plastic poinsettias in the brass urn at his columbarium niche as noon-
time traffic zoomed on Vine Street, recalling that last day, his non-response,
the call that night not an hour after we'd left, his withered body on its side,
still warm, his pain erased. All that's left is an urn-box full of pulverized bones.

An otherwise ordinary day. I tell myself we tried our best, as I am now trying,
like the wild turkeys that spent the night high in my neighbor's trees, flapping
awkward into morning, running along the fence in which they find themselves,
searching for an opening to the creek. Finding their way back into the world.

Crossing A River

The water is wide/I can't cross over.
from a traditional Irish folk song

He was crossing a river before we were aware,
a determination to which we had no access.

If we had only known! Would we have lived different,
knowing how quickly the end would come?

For years he was inching toward that river-edge
we never wanted or imagined, did not think about.

We'd made our wills and directives years before.
We gave no thought to a possible early doom.

After the diagnosis, he wrote some things down, then
began his approach. The separation hasn't quite settled.

I'm still standing here by water moving swiftly south,
hoping to glimpse his white hair amid those dark trees.

I Go Through My Days

I go through my days; life without sparkle.
You're gone; it's difficult to concentrate.
Late summer, I wander out to the night,
Search the sky bowl for some kind of order.

You're gone; I have trouble concentrating.
Life feels flat; even small tasks leave me blue.
My world seems to lack beauty and order,
Until I step out to the silent dark.

When life goes flat, little feels worth doing.
Can there be meaning beyond this blueness?
Is that twinkling star a sign in the dark?
Surely, you'd want me to be happy again.

Meaning must lie beyond what I now feel.
Trees we planted, our house, the life we built.
I know you'd want me to be happy again.
The red of sunsets, cardinals, petunias, fox.

I try to find sparkle in every day.
Shade, shelter, our small family, the love.
I look up at the stars and moon at night,
Breathe in green, as unseen arms hold me up.

Words of Summer

I have no words for the heat, other than it's my least favorite weather.
When summer temps creep into the intolerable, I retreat to my cave.

The first year in our new house we couldn't afford air conditioning,
so each day after work, we turned on fans and headed downstairs.

My yard defies description. Shall we just leave it that the rain this year
grew it to impenetrable portions? That sizeable creatures in it disappear?

Sun. Shade. Fan. Chair. Glass. Green. Tree. Shrub. Vine. Flower.
Limb. Leaf. Weed. Bird feeder. Blue Jay. Woodpecker. Oriole. Fox.

So many shades of green, like early spring and hard summer. I suppose a tribe
in the topics has twenty words for it, but *Roget* and I can only think up eleven.

Here, I should insert that it's been half a year since my husband died.
There are multiple words for grief, but mostly no one wishes to hear.

At Holmes Lake, Mid-May

Last winter the Canada geese waddled on
its ice, thick, chattered in pools of open water,
and small ice-fishing shacks dotted the lake.

A lengthy season, jammed with snow and freezing
and elusive longing. We have moved on to spring,
when spirits lift from the soil and promise renewal.

Today from the top of the dam, a pair of mallards
down on the lake appear to drift, as if without
effort the wind pushes them along from behind.

I wish life was that simple. In the witching hour,
you called my name; I woke in a sweat of grief.
Five months ago, you left us too soon. And yet

evidence of your closeness and being remain.
I am surrounded by your handiwork, but long
for your warmth, as emptiness settles in.

I glide over this plane of earth, carry my blues
just below the water's surface, ever present,
my duck-legs fast-paddling and unseen.

Early Spring

I sit in your chair
Wearing your fleece plaid robe
Drink the coffee I made for one
Stare out back
So much work around here

The dead spruce that fell in a high wind
Its shallow roots dangle
Brittle branches broken, scattered
Holding the trunk up horizontal
Like a stiff giant centipede

Grackles have adapted to seed-eating
Juncos still peck under the feeders
A fox den must be somewhere near
The far corner perhaps under limbs
I see an adult every day

Our neighbors' yards suddenly green
Leaves are sprouted
The daffodils you planted
Are about to bloom
Pollinator garden is waking up

You've been gone for months
But who's counting
My loss is not anyone else's
I must learn to live
Without you

You no longer have my back
You've lost your back-up
Like the comment
Scrawled in a card
Was it meant to comfort?

Which I must let go
This is now my job
Keep moving forward
Smile when you're feeling blue
Be happy even when it's not true

Dead of Night

Don't cry because it's over
Smile because it happened
                    —often attributed to Dr. Seuss

at times in the night I wake
to hear breathing beside me

like a faint shadow following me
into the realness of separation

I used to say you were my better half
we grew from teens into retirement

each better because of the other
now I must learn to live with absence

those unexplained clunks and bumps
nightmares in the dead of night

Mother used to say nothing good
ever happens after midnight

back then a revelation that people
stayed awake past nine o'clock

these days I stay up late rise early
sometimes nap in the afternoon

until my heavy breaths wake me
and beside me a fat cat snores

my days are surrounded by your
presence the shelter we shared

is that you looking over my shoulder
our breaths floating up into the blue?

Light in the Ceiling

Forget logic, improbability,
reason, what sounds plausible I explain
for the faint light on our bedroom ceiling
that for weeks I believed would sustain

me after midnight when I woke to train
my eyes at that odd glow. Never before
seen, I was sure it was you, called in vain
your name after you died. Could it be true?

It's tough to argue the face of belief
or long-held desires. Allow me to say
that each day I think of you in more than
just moments, that this game-change passageway

will someday normalize, will shape and train,
ease doubt. My love for you will never wane.

Stuff People Say

Things happen for a reason.
It was God's will.
God never gives you more than you can handle.
Jesus needed a craftsman in heaven.
He's looking down from heaven.
He's watching over your shoulder.
He's in a better place.
He's still with you.
At least he's not suffering.
You lost your back-up.
It's for the best.
We all die someday.
Melanoma is a beast.
Cancer is a bitch.
Life's a beach, and then you die.
You had a lot of years together!
Cherish the memories!
He was too young.
You are too young.
Life isn't fair.
How are you doing by now?
I didn't know what to say.
I don't know what to say.
I just can't go there.
[Some didn't say a thing.]
[Most never mention it.]
Thoughts and prayers.
Such sad news.
Be good to yourself.
How are you doing, really?
Please take care of yourself.
I'm holding you in my heart.
I can't imagine.
I'm so sorry.
Love and light to you.
Love. And light.

For a While We Could Forget

For a while we could forget about his cancer
Counting cardinals at the feeders in the backyard
Toward twilight as the light dimmed under bare limbs

I counted the males, though females were there, too
Counted blotches of bright red that flitted and
Chased each other from their favored seed

Six, then three, then one, one pair, two pairs, four
Something unseen scattered them all to safeness
He said once, *It feels like the cancer is winning*

I was too scared later to ask him what he saw
After we had given up on the treatments
Squished sideways beside him in the recliner

We watched as one by one birds flew
Until the last male left us, too
Until the blackness came

THREE

My Old Cat

My old cat is dying. His heart still beats
and his chest heaves, but I know what comes soon.

He eyes me in the recliner, noon,
as I mouth food. I think of the pills and treats,

the pricey brand I tried in the small can,
and yet he still shrinks. Every now and then

he tries to rise, but his legs won't stand.
Sprawled on the tile floor, his eyes open,

his body half in shadow half in sun.
I cannot bear to take him to the vet.

They won't be able to change anything, let
alone treat his age, or bring back the fun

he brought to our lives. If I could open
the glass door, let the breeze ruffle his hair,

tickle his nose, I would; I can't go there
in the cold. My cat's death must be his own.

Anniversary

Early: sun attempts to poke through the wall
of green outside my glass door. This, the new door,
new portal to the light we seem to crave, the house
that began modest and somehow grew, like love.

And I guess it is love, the glue that keeps us together,
teens without a clue starting down a jagged path,
proof, perhaps, it's better to travel than to arrive?
Each day we grow further alike, joined at the hip,

and the more things stay the same, how indeed
they change: the home we built, a family raised,
a pasture transformed into woods—wings and fur
and burrowing things now clearly in charge.

What, if anything, do we actually own or need?
We simply carry on—updating, knocking out,
replacing, never uttering the f-word—*finished*,
like our bodies—this life a work in progress.

In the photos, who was that dark-haired man?
When was I ever that waist-length blonde?
We could never sell this place, so many details
left undone, but by now does it even matter?

What can I possibly say, my dear, that is yet unsaid?
Living with you is like the sun that has muscled itself
into this remodeled room, that in searching for father—
who by now you resemble—I have found the light.

Moonlight Meditations

There was full magic streaming in the upstairs
farmhouse windows, enough to call us out
of sleep, stare at the odd silver light washing
over trees, henhouse, silo, clothesline, corncrib,
cattle, fences, hog shed, and ruts in the dirt lane.
Mother hushed us toward beds, but Father
opened his rough hands to ours, walked
us out into that grainy black-and-white film,
to gleams on the gravel, shimmers across
the stock tank, the skewed reflections on
broken windows of the old machine shed.

First it was that cow jumping over the moon,
Mother reading me a picture book, and Father
humming *By the Light of the Silvery Moon*.
Then Sinatra crooned *Fly Me to the Moon*,
which carried us to Beatles' *Mr. Moonlight*,
then Credence and *Bad Moon Rising*,
Stevens' *Moonshadow*, Morrison's *Moondance*,
on to Pink Floyd's *Dark Side of the Moon*:
hard as rock, the vocals, lyrics, guitar licks
that later flowed to our son and friends, teen
believers and full-blast from the basement.

The sun is male, we learn, the moon female—
his yang to her yin, together rotating in a black-
white circle, though nothing is straightforward
about ocean waves, wind, warmth, evaporation,
cloud, storm, lightning, thunder, fire, ashes, soil,
seeds, sprouts, sun, animals, life. What could
possibly go wrong? The blood moon, for example,
thought to be evil; the relentless sun, blazing on.
And is it so, my dear, that our long-time quarrel
can be explained, if not understood? Your heat,
explosion, fire balanced by my cool, dark water?

Does it matter if we're present?
When a tree falls in the forest,
when a cow passes gas in a field,
if no one is gazing at the moon?
So much depends on human perception,
they say. I say: ask ants in the rotted log
of our windbreak if hearing matters;
ask the burrowing woodchuck underground
if it perceives scent; ask the black-gold oriole
belting its spring melody from our treetop
if moonlight helped it migrate to this place.

Some 400 billion years ago, a planetary explosion
created the moon. Luna, the Roman moon
goddess, rode across the sky in a silver chariot.
The Omaha people believe the sun and moon
quarreled, resulting in division: scatter or gather,
direct or follow, walk or sleep, light or dark.
Tonight, the moon at crescent with bright-eyed
Venus beside it could be my father, winking.
Little brown bats flap and swoop for bugs
as this wild acre exhales in the pale light.
I'm a better human breathing the moon.

Full Lunar Eclipse, Late September

We're told this gift of the heavens will not return for eons.
We prepare to receive it, clean out our calendars and hearts,
Stand at the sky-altar facing east and pray for a clear night.

The prairie spreads its gold and purple garments
Over the low hills and onto the undulating Plains.
Here, we breathe the pulse of deep roots, exhale earth.

Cattle settle onto grass, burrowing owls hop
Into ground holes, coyotes and pronghorns
Find cover in time to navigate by the stars.

It will be an eclipse visible to most of North America.
It will be a Super Moon, closest to Earth for decades.
It will be a Red Moon, a hanging reminder of doom.

We're not far from the Black Hills, the place that is
To the Lakota *the heart of everything that is*, the womb
Of Mother Earth, locus of births and sacred burials.

And meanwhile, further east, well into the night
Farmers work their fields, aided by this Harvest Moon,
Before and after it dims yellow, to orange, then blood.

Moon's Big Moment

—Solar eclipse August 21, 2017

A narrow band, a matter of seconds, short
glimpses. Everything blocked, booked, hassled,
and not just for telescopes, cameras, geeks.

So adorable they were, chasers all lined up
in odd spectacles, the lucky ones in the bull's
eye center of my moon shadow, looking up.

Beaches, mountain tops, prairies, and lakes
all crowded, hotels from Oregon to Carolina
were filled, locals displaced, traffic impossible.

Their ancestors thought the world would end.
Now, they connect with others, with something
greater their grandchildren will remember.

At a distance, I could feel the excitement build
as I approached, nothing to stop me, not even
clouds or distractions or disappointments.

And children, with colanders in hand, danced
over half-circles on sidewalks, pranced under
trees, as sunlight through them slowly narrowed.

By chance, over land I aligned perfectly with Earth
to darken the sun for a few daytime minutes.
Below me, stars shone and birds were confused.

The silvery eeriness of the corona, light blocked
by my totality, as if nature was holding its breath.
And for fleeting moments, I was equal to the sun.

The Wrens This Morning

The wrens this morning have decided to scold me
as I move past their house hanging under the eave.

The lake mists and ripples beneath low clouds,
same as the river, ever in motion, its far bank
of trees shrouded in heavy air.

All around me, the earth is in motion: leaves unfold,
orioles buzz-trill, and waves lap against the edges.

After days of hot winds and nighttime storms,
the air is unusually calm. We have gathered here
under silent limbs for a brief lifetime—

wings in motion, waters alive, as the planet
exhales—to breathe as one.

Another Word for Love

Sixteen and sunny and the yellow orb rises
                                    in the south

because I'm always turned around at this cabin on the river
where this morning ice chunks more like oversize slush piles

move swift while others gather like turtles on sandbars, all
curving eastward to the Missouri—wide and flat,

                                        silent trunks
and sheltered geese on the far side alive, co-witness to this going—

globs of snow from somewhere many counties upstream, and
I wonder how many words the Pawnee had for snow,

                                            like
that dry two inches I swept this morning with little effort,

not the snow-rain-ice I struggled with a few of weeks ago,
and now, I warm with coffee and count the passing seconds

of winter's hour-glass at its middle, the unburrowed groundhog
several states east of us not seeing his shadow, and why not

            believe in a small mammal tossing his forecast
into the storm of prognosticators, so inexact and charming,

who might have another name for this floating scene, this small
gathering here

            warmed by stories and hearts, the tender way years
of huddling together have bonded us almost as close as blood.

Poem of the Heart

this poem of the heart is near the river
where water at night glistens in moonlight
moon at three-quarters a nibbled cookie
the cookies we nibble from the pile
the pile of food when we gather

our gathering on the river to write
writing in notebooks, art books, laptops
files, folders fat with poems and stories
stories about lovers both lost and found
lovers of language and food and water

the lake water still in the dark
dark sky with a ring around the moon
moon yellow like harvest cornstalks
yellow moon faithful, illuminating our walk
walking to claps of cottonwood leaves

walking and talking and taking it all in
talk of children, grandchildren, life
our lives and the ones now lost
the lost now on the pages we write
we write them alive and what they meant

what we mean by choosing what to say
what we say and what we leave out
leaving out what's not important
we choose, we construct what's important
when we construct our poems and stories

our stories that go out into the world
the world takes in our stories, or not
it's not their taking them in, it's the writing
for the sake of art, Earth, fairness
the writing arts that keeps us sane

the insanity that's taken over the country
our country heading somewhere wrong
wrong direction, wrong people, wrong
this will take more than two rights to correct
it will take a shipload of rights

so hard now to turn around this ship
the Earth cannot afford them to win
when winning is for only the few
thank god for laws protecting us
our water, air, land, all creatures

we will not let them take it all
the black of night, the bright of moon
the river, the lake, the water
our poems of sadness, beauty, and heart
our stories of redemption

our lives, our lovers, our language

River Music

Snow crystals fly as we drive to the river,
Baring trees near the highway in frigid air.
Women—with our sorrows, laughs, and hungers—
Cabin-gather, focus on love and words.

Limbs move bare near the river in the wind.
We bring notepads, laptops, and books, gather
To feed each other more than love and words.
Snow-covered ice mostly hides the channel.

We use notepads, laptops, books, to gather
Our voices, pen our lines, collect our thoughts.
Snow-ice clouds the open water channel,
Geese in the distance dark against the white.

Our voices, lines, thoughts are honored here,
Laughing together layer into layer.
At dusk, geese become one with the far bank,
Poems and stories leap on screens and paper.

We listen to each one's deep-held layer,
This practice of knowing and not knowing.
Poems, stories take shape on screens and paper.
Our music, immersion in lovely words.

We practiced how to know while not knowing.
The geese rose loud, at once, off the river.
Our music sung, our voices spent, on words.
None of us wanted to leave at the end.

Women satisfied sorrows, laughs, hungers.
Ground-snow held as we drove from the river.

Salt Creek, Early Morning

suddenly I invade a sanctuary

beneath the footbridge
two then four
dark-hued ducks lift
and flap down the creek

I departed the cozy bed
the heated house
to greet daybreak
my own method

flat water mirroring sky
all else remaining colorless
sandbars snags
banks thick with wild grass

they move from harm an easy distance
mates perhaps pintails maybe
lighting into perfect circle-pairs
radiating over the shallows

much of this day
I'll get paid to care
about other business
offering my small twigs

yet even indoors I'll glance out
over clean treetops sense the sun
over my desk detect the echo
of small voices wing-like

and later in our warm nest
describing that walk in the cold
the pairs of ducks
their quiet dash

the instinct we all return to

Loving Wide Open

Loving wide open spaces, like Flatirons
butting up against the Rocky Mountains,
overlooking the dry plains toward the east,

like hands that say stop speaking—be glad
your real life right now is in the more humid
region with its green prairies and flat streams,

close enough you can drive away from
in one day—stare at rocks jutting into sky,
watch rain clouds build in the afternoon,

then spill coolness through the screen,
waking you from the nap you deserve after
trudging your flatland feet one by one upward

on the paths, the well-used incline that leaves
you so breathless you must stop every few
yards or so, inhale it again, to where

jays and squirrels chatter from pines, and, if
you're lucky, where a few deer make their way
sure-footed across rocks away from you,

on the switchbacks now in shade, the vista
overlooking the city and those far
distances in the haze of summer, places

that now feel like a far-off dream, the dream
under stars you're closer to by a mile,
stars if we bother to listen, moment

to moment, and learn to love in the dark.

Blackbirds Lined Up on a Fence

Between the Tetons and Wind River mountains,
unmoving crows sit on a black wet fence.

Rain and snow; wispy cloud-shawls
hug the foothills. Herefords and hay rolls
out-number humans. A flatbed truck delivers
dinner to a half-dozen horses trotting toward it.

The rain and the snow and the road
are indistinguishable. Off to one side,
a dead cow is down but not yet bloated.

In Jackson Hole, no one is hungry: No soup
kitchen, no homeless shelter, nothing ugly.
Off the main drag, a motel sign: *Rooms
to accommodate everyone's budget.*

Yesterday, Sunday, could sundown
behind Grand Teton have been anything
short of gorgeous?
The snow and the blackbirds are one.
The murder of crows is one.

On the official Wyoming map, Continental
Divide pass trails included: *Indians, explorers,
fur trappers, soldiers, prospectors, hunters,
settlers; Gros Ventre Range; Shoshone National
Forest; Wind River Reservation; Sand Creek
Massacre Trail.*

In Jackson, stone and timber homes
half way up the foothills fix glassed gazes
toward the Tetons.

Inside the cab, warm, we pilot a pickup
powered by the pumped-up hundreds-of-millions-
of-years-ago remains of all that was once alive.

A single crow shakes snow
off its black wing.

Sun breaks through, and the valley widens
into the Great Divide Basin. Prairie schooners
and the Pony Express sped through this sagebrush
toward the next mountain range and the next,
toward their promise, their destiny.

This speech is disputed—does it matter?
Chief Seattle, in surrendering native lands,
once said: *The earth does not belong to us.*
We belong to the earth.

It was sunny all that afternoon. Behind us,
it was snowing and would continue to snow.
Blackbirds sat on the pressure-treated wood.

At the Prairie Celebration

—weekend after 9/11

Heavy mist of grief in the
afternoon on the tall grass while
green canopies dot the hillsides.

Far from the city, we move in silence
on the mowed path, as dampness
rises from deep and complicated roots.

Learn insect and bird, seine the pond
for anything alive, seedheads and wild
flower stalks waving us forward.

Virgin, unplowed acres an island
surrounded by corn fields, everything
now known as *before* and *after.*

While rain clatters the shed roof,
we gather to hear the refuge of place,
acknowledge a changed world.

Mercy rains down our faces as
a recovered raptor—*for the all dead*—
is released into an uncertain sky.

After, we heed cries of gratitude
from the distant and tallest of oaks.
Healing comes on muffled steps.

Taking Down the Tree

I took down the dry-needled tree one ornament at a time,
packed each away—Garfield in a Santa hat, gaudy round balls,

tin bells, stuffed reindeer, stars, angels, family photo ornaments—
the gilded treasures and shiny accumulations of a lifetime—

while I listened to *A Charlie Brown Christmas*, sang along with
the children's chorus to "Christmas Time" and "Hark the Herald,"

then wept like Snoopy as The Flying Ace, when Schroeder
on his tiny grand plinked out patriotic, then sad tunes of WWI,

and recalled those years when the young girls helped me decorate,
unwrapped each ornament, their sweet-breath ohs and ahs, same

as they now discover each life pleasure, one at a time, though they
may one day be melancholy in the tasks of grown-ups, yet satisfied,

as perhaps Vince Guaraldi was as he blazed into the world of jazz,
his "Cast Your Fate to the Wind" both an uplift and a downdraft,

those children growing into their own skins, airing their own music,
dancing with abandon like "Linus and Lucy," their own bright baubles

hanging on display in spite of how we know it can all change, by
by choice or lucky accident, the tiny moves we make toward love.

January

            and the waterfowl can't decide
whether to stay or go. Blame it on an earlier

balmy December. They move about—field to creek
to lake, overhead some heading north, some south—

in vees and yous and whys, according to the six-year-old.
I stare at the long undulating lines and cannot disagree.

According to the news, there are too many geese, their
numbers soon to decrease by disease and open season.

I ponder this on a walk beside the highway, my mind split
by a conversation in each ear—noisy machinations

from the geese-covered field, whine from hundreds
of tires on the four-lane—wondering which one is saner.

By now they are everywhere, especially near water—
stubble fields, empty lots, back yards—black heads,

goosenecks, honking and craning and shuffling, a few
mallards keeping company in a puddle next to the street.

Later, we stop with the car windows down—study
green duck heads, blue speculum on duck wings—

so close we can almost touch. And from the back seat
the quiet six-year-old arrives at her best response:

Quack! you sillies! Quack! Quack! Quack! Quack!
Quack!

I Met Him in Math Class

Good girls go to heaven, bad girls
go everywhere. —Mae West

When I met him in math class, I did not meet him,
exactly; rather, I muscled my heart toward the hot
pursuit of desire, that elusive candle flittering
the dingy hallways like Tinkerbell,

                            spreading sparks
from a wand that landed on the lanky athletes,
the book nerds, even on the antsy freshmen
who multiplied near the army-green lockers,

our marble floors overrun with culture clash and baby
boomers, our teachers mostly prudish and no-nonsense,
some old veterans who took pleasure in teasing the girls,
my face flushed at unwanted attention,

                         so I plunged even
further into algebra, geometry, then trig, but the struggle
inside myself would not quit: that longing and no clue—
should I elevate my brain or listen to other body leads,

squeaky-clean or join the bad girls, and whatheheck did that
mean anyway? With an abundance of caution, I calculated:
pursuit pocked with restraint, I tiptoed to high school dances—
Keen-Time! —showed up at his gymnastics practice,

                            walked
home by his house, glanced sideways at the exact second—
hope-hope-hoping that trail of sparkled dust would smack
him and me simultaneously, then burst into flames.

Farm Dog

He never came inside the house: Pets
belonged outdoors, no furry creatures were
allowed to sooth our disturbing dreams at night.

Before I came along, earlier dogs were more
beloved than Brownie: Ching, a chow, and
Yankee, who chased cars on the gravel road.

The mutt became my pal when my brothers
left home: A time of great change, unrest,
escalation, and an unpopular war that loomed.

Not many noticed the beginnings of the end: The
emptying out of small towns, the farm consolidations.
As we struggled, Earl Butz said, *Get big, or get out.*

In grainy photos: I'm ten or so, in a summer dress
next to the windmill, gripping Brownie's neck,
grinning, his mangy hair not clearly visible, and

in the next I'm a teen with cat-eye specs holding
a purse, modeling the skirt and blouse I sewed,
dreaming of being someplace, anyplace else.

In-between: Dad decided to quit farming and learn
a new trade. Those days blurred by. When the dog
died under the porch, it took us a week to find him.

Riding Horses

Susan had horses and luckily, she and I were
cousins, our parents got along, and I could
stay overnight at her house sometimes
if our mothers said yes, if I did all the tasks
that would give me a night away, which is a lie,

because I had no tasks, I kept my room clean
and Mother never expected me to do a thing,
which is not necessarily a good thing, because
when I married, I really had no idea how
to clean a toilet or boil water,

but seriously, it was all so strange at Susan's
house, food tasted different, gravy stuck
to the roof of my mouth, and Christmas cookies
snatched from waxed paper in the freezer a treat,

and I loved riding atop one of her mares,
as we took off over hills in the pasture
and rode down gravel roads and into farmyards,
like one of the boys I was most interested in,

his farm nothing like ours, junky, low buildings
and chickens running free in the muddy farm yard,
his family had to wear four-buckle over-boots
to walk anywhere, something we only wore
when it rained or snowed, and when we rode

up the lane he and his sister were carrying egg
baskets to the house, this boy with the red hair
and freckles I was pretty sure I was in love with,
his hazel eyes and easy smile, his husky frame,

and later in Susan's bed with the lights off
she told me how one time she had crawled into
her parent's bed and for some reason her mother
left the room and how her sleepy father
rolled over and grabbed her in that place

between her legs while she pretended to sleep,
and he woke up with a start and muttered *oh no*,
or something like that, and then I don't remember
what, maybe rolled over back to sleep again,
and I thought about that and how I was sore there,

in that place between my legs from riding the horses
I wasn't used to, and those horses, their muscular
firm haunches and sturdy legs, my swaying in the saddle,
its smooth leather and its earthy scent, clutching
the horn and reins, a summer wind through my hair,

and how I sometimes wondered about Susan
and her father and how probably nothing was ever
said after that, like love and so many other things
that happen when we're young never are.

Bay of Pigs

—the failed invasion of Cuba, 1961

That next fall, Billy Anderson,
eighth grader at our country school,
stood up at recitation and said

Russians have nuclear warheads
pointed at SAC and we have the same
pointed at them

and if things get really bad
they will all be fired off
and we're all gonna die.

His face had a sort of smug look.
A second-grade girl started to cry.
Mrs. Swanson told him to sit down.

She dabbed her eyes with a hanky,
as she did whenever "war" came up:
her brother died in the Battle of the Bulge,

and none of us knew what to say.
Cuba was a long way away, and the Bay
of Pigs sounded like a soupy hog pen.

Cold war felt surreal, unlike
those storied battlegrounds our dads
returned home from to farm again.

That fall, for a thirteen-day eon,
we feared spy plane and naval blockade,
sky-watched for red missiles of death.

At recess, on swings and teeter-totters,
we heard B-52 bombers droning back
to headquarters, flying over our farms,

to where we were glad to return
to our everyday lives, back to our chores,
fields and supper tables

and into the nights where everyone
was asleep except for me, up to my neck
in flannel and wool, the furnace hissing,

as bare branches moved in moonlight,
while frost crystals nucleated over
the windows to form odd patterns,

trying not to picture what could happen—
to family, barn, silo, cattle, and pets—in
a flash more brilliant than all imagination.

The Moon Keeps Her Secrets

There was that ride home from town, the back seat
of the old Chrysler, the sky navy-dark, a vigilant moon
following us, rounded, steady, silent.

And the news: missing high-school drop-out, her body
found near the road in the field we were about to pass,
when my brother yelled *BOO!* and I screamed.

How many times we'd passed that place not knowing,
how many phases of moon crossed over it for months,
the rain, the wind, the frozen snowdrifts.

She lay where someone dumped her body next to
the fence line trees, where in spring a low sickle bar
revealed her face, by then as blank as the witness moon.

Afterward—the sheriff, state patrol, scuttlebutt—the field
continued to grow alfalfa. My brother and his buddies
found bits of hair, fiber, comb, dared each other to touch.

Oldest homicide in this state unsolved. Somewhere,
someone long-gone by now knew what happened,
the nightmare that rose up to an unblinking moon.

That Summer Night

That summer night, moonless, when I was six
my father and I walked from the yellow kitchen
down steps and sidewalk past the windmill, milk barn
corn crib, cattle pens, to the dirt lane near the rusted,

unused implements parked next to the windbreak
filled with crickets and cicadas as breeze through pines
whispered for attention, toward the county road

to view stars teeming above the curve of land, which
I could not see except for the most brilliant, the curve
of my eyeballs too severe, nearsighted, but what
I remember most was my father's warm hand,

his other pointing to a vastness that neither of us
could fathom, his voice hushed, with whiffs of manure-
dirt from the hog shed, the occasional grunt-squeal,
and while cottonwood leaves clapped in approval.

About the Author

Twyla M. Hansen was Nebraska's State Poet in 2013-2018, and received the 2021 Nebraska Literary Heritage Award, among others. Her previous books won Nebraska Book Awards and WILLA Literary Awards. Her writing is published recently in *Prairie Schooner, Briar Cliff Review, South Dakota Review, More in Time: A Tribute to Ted Kooser, Nebraska Poetry: A Sesquicentennial Anthology 1867-2017*, and websites Academy of American Poets, Poetry Foundation, Poetry Out Loud, and more. Twyla grew up on land in northeast Nebraska her grandparents farmed as immigrants from Denmark.

Acknowledgments

"Another Word for Love," "Distant Stars Are Calling to Me," "Orioles," and "Under the Sun" in *South Dakota Review*, 2022.

"Farm Dogs," "Full Lunar Eclipse," and "The Moon Keeps Her Secrets" in *Oakwood Magazine*, 2022

"Full Lunar Eclipse, Late September" online #NASAMoonSnap https://www.facebook.com/hashtag/nasamoonsnap (accessed 20Aug2022)

"Garbage, Etc." in *Briar Cliff Review*, 2021.

"I Never Thought I'd Outlive My Pine Trees" in *More in Time: A Tribute to Ted Kooser*. Editors Marco Abel, Timothy Schaffert, and Jessica Poli (University of Nebraska Press, 2021).

"I Carry the Grief" in *Gatherings: an art and poetry-based experiment in giving and receiving* (Gatherings Project online, 2020).

"Moonlight Meditations" in *The Night's Magician: Poems About the Moon*. Editors Philip C. Kolin and Sue Brannan Walker (Negative Capability Press, 2018).

"January" and "Salt Creek, Early Morning" in *Sanctuary Near Salt Creek*, a limited-edition chapbook (Lone Willow Press, 2001).

Notes

The poem by May Sarton (1912-1995) is "A Prayer" (harvardsquarelibrary. org). She was an award-winning poet, novelist, and memoirist.

"The Wrens this Morning," "Another Word for Love," "Poem of the Heart," and "River Music" are for my camper-writer sisters: Barbara Schmitz, Christy Hargesheimer, Karen Shoemaker, Kelly Madigan, Lynda Madison, Lucy Adkins, Marge Saiser, Mary Pipher, Pam Barger, Shelly Geiser, and Suzanne Kehm.

"Blackbirds Lined Up on a Fence," is inspired by Wallace Steven's poem, "Thirteen Ways of Looking at a Blackbird" in Harmonium (Knopf, 1923).

The quote by William Faulkner, "The past is never dead. It is not even past," is from his novel Requiem for a Nun (Random House, 1951).

And, as always, I am grateful for the love and support of my long-time Prairie Trout writing pals/ uber-talented friends Pam Herbert Barger, Mary Pipher, Marjorie Saiser, and Karen Gettert Shoemaker.